The Archangel's Pen Presents

"The Journey Within"

Book I

Of The Collection:

"Archangel Michael Speaks"

Written & Channeled By

Carolyn Ann O'Riley

3rd Edition

Edited By Carolyn Ann O'Riley

All correspondence and inquires
should be directed to:
Carolyn Ann O'Riley
The Archangel's Pen
18794 Vista Del Sol
Dallas, Texas 75287-4023 USA
214-232-7199 Phone
E-mail: channel333@sbcglobal.net
http://www.carolynannoriley.com

Library Of Congress Catalog Card Number: 00-190259
2000 1st Edition: ISBN 1-891870-10-6
2006 2nd Edition: ISBN 1-4116-7931-8
2013 3rd Edition: ISBN 978-1-4116-7931-3

Dedication

This is dedicated to The Creator and
The Creator's Messenger, Archangel Michael,
for their infinite love, faith and Omni-presence.
Also to my Guardian Angels for their
Love, protection, vigilance and constant nudging.

To all of my Family both through blood and
through Light for their love, may they truly know how very special
they are to me.

To the devoted subscribers of Archangel Michael's Messages
Remember you are loved beyond measure.

Author's Acknowledgment

I have been very blessed to have had these messages of love and hope channeled through me for your understanding and enjoyment.

My desire for you is to share the love that has been channeled through me so that it may speak directly to your heart, for your own discernment and validation.

The Creator's message is that we learn to love ourselves so that we may remember how to love others.

In our remembrance, of The Creator's love for each of us we can remember who we truly are and from whence we came.

We can change the world one person at a time through love.

Love is all there is.

Table of Contents

"The Journey Within"

Book I

Of the Collection

"Archangel Michael Speaks"

Written & Channeled by

Carolyn Ann O'Riley

Chapter 1

December 15, 1993 I picked up a silk brown paisley covered journal and wrote" The snow is now falling in place of the rain. Big fluffy flakes of white lace tumbling from the Heavens."

I'd been given the book many years ago and never picked it up until that day and that was all I wrote that day.

July 11, 1994 I wrote: "The entity came again last night that icy cold draft with the paralyzing Vibrational field. It turned me physically on my left side this time, facing towards my sleeping husband. I heard the male voice saying, "You don't need this" as the massive currents of Vibrational energy, poured through my body. I couldn't move just as before, totally paralyzed until the energy ceased. After the energy ceased the symbols and pictures, something recognizable like memos and written documents went flashing through my mind to quickly to grasp what they really were".

It took me a while to figure out what this was all about. I know now that it was my wakeup call from Archangel Michael. The first time the energy came several weeks before, I obviously was far too afraid to understand that this energy was pure love and the source Divine. Archangel Michael had used this beautiful energy transfusion, if you will, to elevate my Vibrational fields so that I might begin remembering and hearing my awakening guidance as he showed me my path. It was time now to begin the Journey Within and reclaim all that was truly mine.

I've been asked many times how do you know it's Archangel Michael and my answer is, I just know, He has been with me always.

This has been a glorious journey of inner work filled with many triggers of remembrance.

The mission within these pages is to tweak your own desire to go further on your spiritual path and share the tools and steps that Archangel Michael has suggested to assist you on your journey of remembrance.

As I cognizantly began my remembrance journey I realized that I'd been on this path since I arrived within this incarnation, but blind folded if you will.

One of Archangel Michael's directives for this book and in the next two volumes was to share my own insights and Angel stories along with his messages. Archangel Michael desired to place this book as the first in a collection of three that will be produced.

His directive helped me understand that we are receiving many many things that we do not recognize as Divine knowledge and Messages from our Angels. I have found it helpful to allow my guidance to show me other writings as confirmations at times. These confirmations always lead to the triggers of Ah Ha! I have sensed that Archangel Michael desired for you to have a similar opportunity by reading some of my experiences within these pages.

So my sharing begins with your knowing that my inner senses and Angelic nudging decided that it was time that I begin this journey and remember my own Angelic connections.

My Mom was terminally ill and as she sensed her own transformation time approaching she began reading Mary Summer Rain's "No Eyes" books. She found them fascinating although she wasn't sure why, but this was what she was drawn to. She loaned me one of her books.

I thought to myself this isn't something that I wanted to read when she handed me the book. I put it down for a day or two and was reminded of it again, I can't remember how.

I picked the book back up and began to read. It stimulated my thirst for reading about the Native Americans. The rituals, the Shaman ways seemed to be bringing me back to a memory of some of my past life experiences. I ordered all the books that Mary Summer Rain had written then and shared them all with my Mom. I bought several more Native American Indian paperbacks relating to the very first tribes and could almost see myself within the pages.

I've since seen a picture, in a flyer ,advertising books, about the history of the Native American Indian tribes, of a Native American Indian Woman that looked very familiar to me as if I were looking at my own photograph.

The next direct step was my trip to the Barnes and Noble bookstore to just browse and look for books about Angels. Why Angels? It just seemed to be what I wanted to read about. Of course at that time I was foolish enough to think that that was my idea, I now know how and why this happens. Finding a plethora of books really made it hard to decide which one to buy, but my guidance knew exactly and made sure that I brought the correct book home by Terry Lynn Taylor.

My family doesn't share my passion for my spiritual pursuits, so we have an understanding that I allow them their journey and they allow me mine, so when the house was quiet and others had gone off to bed, I pulled my book from the bookstore bag and sat down at the kitchen table to read a few pages before I went to bed myself.

The day had been a long hard one, my eyes were really tired but I felt driven to read some that night. I opened to the first chapter and began reading. Then I noticed something really odd about the page. The word Angel was spelled out within the printed paragraph letters diagonally in both directions across the page. It made an "X" from page border to page border spelling the word "Angel" in each direction. I looked at it again and it was still there. I smiled to myself and thanked the Angels because I knew then and there that I had invited them into my life by my intention and I welcomed their presence in my life. The Angels were communicating with me and it was wonderful. I've opened the same book many times after that evening and have never found the

phenomenon to be there again. It was that first special moment of Ah Ha!
contact from HOME and it felt so good.
Several weeks had passed and I'd not had any really unusual happenings. I
spilled something on my shirt at lunch one day. When I arrived at home I
took off the shirt and sprayed it with a stain remover and sat the shirt on top
of the washer within our utility room located next to the kitchen.

The next morning upon arising I went into the utility room to pick up my pet
food bowls to feed our kitties and was drawn to the washer top and the shirt.
The area on the shirt that was stained was glowing and as I picked up the
shirt to look closer the stain remover had formed a heart shape. The heart
shape encompassed the exact location of my heart when the shirt was worn. I
knew that the Angels were communicating with me again. It gave me such a
warm feeling of love to know that I was being looked after by such wondrous
Beings.

Much was going on within my life within a several year time span. My Mom
was dying but slowly and her care required more and more of my efforts and
physical and emotional support. It was like being on a roll-a-coaster with
death and life being the pikes and valleys that spanned the moments of her
existence. I was working full time in a stressful job environment. I wasn't
satisfied with my profession so I was looking for alternatives. My paternal
grandmother was not doing well either. My daughter was going through a
divorce. My son was going to school elsewhere and trying to start his own
business. Needless to say it was a stressful time. The Angels helped me get
through it. I continued to find the books that I was guided to buy and began
putting into practice those exercises that resonated with me.

Each morning I was drawn to open my journal and jot down a few things
whether it was the Angel card that I had drawn that day or whatever. I made
a commitment to myself to set aside a few minutes each morning before I
dashed off to work. These were my quiet moments of meditation and prayer
everyone else had already departed for their day. The poems began to come as I
started this morning ritual.

I took these moments to practice what I had been working on. These were not lengthy periods less than 30 minutes most of the times before I left for work myself each day.

On January 15, 1995 my grandmother passed away. My husband wasn't able to drive with me to the funeral in Vicksburg, Mississippi. I decided being the independent and assertive woman that I am, that I would drive myself. The day started off well, I got into the car and began my 400-mile drive to my grandmother's funeral. I noticed that as I left town the traffic was building rapidly but there was a very unusual cloud formation that my attention was drawn to. Across the sky was a pattern that looked like a wooden window cornice with scalloped edges. Just one long band like that all across the horizon. I've never figured out what the significance of that was, but it has stuck in my memory of that day. The drive time seemed to just whisk right by. I made a mental note of the road construction in the Shreveport area and just listened to the radio and drove. I arrived first in the early afternoon before any of the other family members had reached the agreed upon motel. I lay down on the bed and tried take a short nap. That didn't last long as the family began to arrive one by one.

The funeral was well attended and I was at peace with my grandmother's passing. She had been ill for some time now; she had lived a full life. My Aunt and Uncle came unexpectedly and it was like a prayer answered. I had felt like I was in a huge room with strangers until their presence. You see the Angels also know when we need support the most and make sure that it is provided.

I began the drive home the next morning. The day was gray and there had been rain sprinkles off and on. I had arrived back at the Shreveport construction area again. The side of the road heading back to Texas was in worse condition than the South side of the highway had been. The construction on this North side had no right shoulder, no lines on the road; there was only one small lane open that was next to a concrete barrier. The rain began to pour down. In the blink of an eye the rain was coming down so hard you could not see at all. There was nowhere to pull off the road, the traffic was heavy and you couldn't see. I panicked, my fears were running away with me. I mentally

11

called out to The Creator for help; I just didn't know how I was going to get home in this. Instantly a car appeared in front of me with its red taillights flashing. I knew that my prayers had been answered. That car remained in front of me until the rain stopped about 5 miles ahead. The white car that had been my guide pulled off into the roadside park and vanished. Thanks to The Creator's answering my prayer and The Angels, I arrived back home safe and sound.

I had gone to several physic fairs and really found very little that was answered there. However I decided to try one more time. I gave myself a goal of three readings. I felt that I was drawn to this fair for some reason. All three readings came up empty handed. One of the readers also did hypnotherapy and I had an inner knowing that something within a session with this individual could assist me in my process. I made the appointment. I felt completely comfortable with this individual and really had no idea what to expect. I had never been through a hypnosis session before. I reclined in a reclining chair and he covered me with a light blanket. He took my list of questions that I wanted answers to. Then he slowly began helping me relax through his voice and count down and taking me deeper and deeper within myself while with his mental visualization descriptions raised my Vibrational levels higher and higher. I was not uncomfortable with this process and was at no time without cognizance of what was transpiring to me or around me.

When my physical body was sufficiently relaxed and ready he requested that my higher self-merge with my body. This request was honored and I felt an immediate surge of Vibrational energy enter my body. It was so strong that it felt very much like I was standing in a puddle of water holding onto an electrical cord that was plugged in. There was no pain associated with this sensation but it was a very different feeling. I could feel myself shaking all over with the surges of the energy. I could even sense my eyelids fluttering from the surges.

He assisted me to remember by Father sexually abusing me when I was three. This session was a blessing for it allowed me to begin the releasing process necessary to heal these occurrences. The balance of the questions were answered and He brought me back into my awakened state. The energy subsided as I returned to my awareness, and I felt at peace and ready to deal with my healing steps. He stated he had never worked or seen anyone with that level of intense Vibrational energy entering his or her physical body before. I had nothing that I really compared it to until I remembered and began to understand the connection between this energy transfusion and my much more intense initial two visits from Archangel Michael.

That particular physic fare also brought me into contact with an individual that owned a metaphysical bookstore and taught Reiki. I went through the first and second Reiki Degrees and found that this triggered yet another memory. The Reiki wasn't the healing method that I was really drawn to but the exercise assisted in helping me remember and realize my own method of healing through color from my Atlantis Period. It brought forth visions that relayed that I had been a healer in other life times. This was a gift of remembering another piece of my past life progression, but healing was not meant to be part of my present mission as I understand it during this incarnation; however I've used it.

Through the bookstore I attended a Full Moon meditation that brought me into contact with a wonderful lady that taught a class on Enjoying Abundance with Your Angels. The teacher of this class had a beautiful soothing voice and guided us within to tap into our own spiritual information through meditation.

During this time frame I received my first written channeled message other than poetry from Archangel Michael, April 2, 1996. I was drawn to turn to the computer at work and the following came forth: " As I watch you the words come easy, you are love. All that is love is joy. All that is joy is God. All that is God is love. Be still and know that you are God. Be not afraid change is constant and never ending. You are an instrument in God's plan. You are a key figure in God's blueprint. All will be made known as the time becomes right for each insight. You will be ready. You are learning so rapidly. Be patient with yourself and others. All is for your highest good and the good of all concerned. We are here to serve you, ask us for help when you need it. Be ready to write and work for this Planet's highest good. All is well. You are in our hands and we will never leave you. We helped birth you into this universe and we have been with you ever since through all your previous lives and this

13

one. God has a special place just for you. The time is near. We love you.
Archangel Michael."

This message brought such joy to my heart. I knew that my mission was to
write. I had remembered my name Noeol, when Archangel Michael whispered
it into my ear during a meditation one night, now also remembering my
mission as well, this was a prayer answered. The pieces were coming together.

I began to work with all the principals of release that were being presented to
me one at time. The more that I worked the more awareness and insights came
forth. Through my meditation I began the process of clearing each relationship
and area that no longer served me. When I first began this process one
morning as I released a piece I heard a tinkling bell. The Angels were cheering
me on, but also on that same morning within that same session they let me
know that once I release something it is gone there is no need to carry it with
me and try to release it again.

Not only was I gifted with tinkling bells but also given very unusual lessons.
As I meditated one morning my attention was drawn to the white candle that
was lit. The candle flame was split into two flames but joined as one at the
base. It danced and twirled and split into three flames still joined at the base.
There was such joy watching this dance and such love. I knew that The
Creator was giving me a lesson in Oneness.

In May on the Earth Plane human front, my life was becoming more and
more stressed. My Mother's transition was becoming more imminent and my
younger cousin dropped dead literally no signs or warning. Because my Mom
was in the hospital I couldn't go to my cousin's out of town funeral. I felt
really bad but prayed that all would understand. We later moved Mom into a
nursing home.

On June 27th, 1996 I received a call from the nursing home to come
immediately that my Mom would probably not make it through the day. I
stayed by her bedside day and night until her final cross over on the afternoon
of June 29, 1996. My brother and I would leave only to bath and change
clothes. There was very little sleep during this time. I would arrive home hop

14

into my Jacuzzi tub and allow the warm water to rush over me. I'd meditate for a few moments and Archangel Michael would hand me two golden goblets of some type of golden elixir during my brief meditations, I'd dress and go back to my mother's dying side. Archangel Michael and the golden elixir sustained me during those days of no sleep and intense drama.

Around 2:00 AM on the morning of June 29th my attention was drawn to my Mother's heaving chest. I noticed there two small blue bubbles type shapes that seemed to be intertwined into one. One blue bubble was larger than the other. Afterwards we noticed that my Mom seem to be at peace still struggling with all the bodily functions but her demeanor was at peace. I have since learned that these were in fact her Angels assisting her soul to leave her body to take her spirit home. It took until 1:30PM that afternoon for her physical body to cease but the women we had called Mom left at 2:00AM.

On July 9, 1996 I experienced a blinding flash of light as I was sleeping. This energy pattern, as I later understood, had been building all week as I found it had affected my automobile's electrical dashboard system (my car had been checked out twice that week by the auto shop for all dash lights coming on), and it had disrupted two computers one of which had a hard drive crash, the other simply expired.

During this episode I was also shown my Mother. What I have come to understand from what I saw was, she had not completely decided that she had transitioned she was confused and when I spoke to her and told her she no longer was on the Earth Plane it allowed her the opportunity to finish her transition, which she did in front of my sleeping eyes.

The flash of light was associated with a sucking feeling and I was taken out of my body and entered an unknown realm where my contracts were pulled and shown to me. I was told that one of my missions had been completed which involved my Mother. I was asked to sign new papers. I remember nothing about what the papers contained and remember afterwards that the papers were sucked back up right out of my hands.

I continued with my daily work and joined with several group meditations. I found that I could tell when the energy was flowing into my body, because it would give me a physical headache.

On my first attempt at a group meditation I followed the directions that were provided for joining all the others all over the globe. It was very exhilarating. When I finished I was casually laying on my bed for some reason and three golden circles each with a different Mandela graced my vision one at a time very rapidly.

The meditations and group focus of the 11:11 was another really enlightening one for me. I had meditated during the AM portion of the 11:11 but the PM portion of this time frame proved to be a very different vision. I had been asleep and awakened at 11:11PM to begin my meditation. I noticed that my eyelids didn't want to stay open and I felt like I had no live energy in my body, I couldn't move at all. My awareness was drawn to the left corner of my bedroom that had been filled with golden white light and there in that corner was the vision of a tree encircled with light. I couldn't move or keep my eyes open but I knew this was a special sign for me to have answered when the moment came for me to know it's meaning.

As I have stated before my lessons come in very unusual ways and impart very deep meanings and insights into how the Universe really works. Another such lesson came one day while driving to work. I passed a pond where many mornings I watched the ducks and geese swim as I drove by. It brought me such joy to watch their grace. This morning however I noticed a goose in the road that someone had killed with a car. It just sent my anger in a whirl and I was telling my Angels how horrible this individual was that killed the beautiful goose. The Angels didn't allow me to continue very long before sharing with me that this incident created cords with nasty hooks that connected me to the one that actually killed the goose. They taught me that morning that each judgment binds us to the one that we are judging. The Angels also showed me that there is more to it than the outcome was reflecting. They had contacted this individual's higher self and found out that the person hit the goose accidentally and was very very very upset about the death. I knew instantly that my judgment had only made the matter worse with my added *hook into that person for something that had happened unintentionally. I allowed my Angels to help me release my judgment and ask the person's forgiveness for making the hasty analysis.*

I've had several lessons that actually took place within my office. Archangel Michael actually blew a completely shut door open to bring me the answer I had asked for, after I had dismissed the fire alarm that had gone off one day as a coincidence.

A touch of my hand by Archangel Michael to have me notice the beautiful cardinal that was looking into my office window was another. The cardinal was looking directly into my eyes just as you would glare into someone's soul through their eyes.

The Creator shared with me a lesson about the tree and its flexibility when I was being limiting, ridged and concerned about funds one day.

I've been gifted with numerous answers and insights in the most unusual settings and places. Being told I am loved as I slept, hearing the words you are a prophet on a trip to my favorite place, the mountains. Having my great uncle bid me goodbye when I was 10 years old by seeing his vision in a circle of light after his passing. My stove timer going off the morning that my maternal grandmother passed on. I could sense when my Father was thinking about me during his life as well as after his death because of a specific tingle in the palm of my right hand..

The point of all these insights is to have you understand that they come when you give your intent that it is time for you to progress on to the next rung of the spiral of your evolutionary ladder. The Angels come when you invite them into your life to bring you joy, protection, information and messages of all types.

When the moment of awakening is appropriate for you the suggestions, visions, pictures, symbols, words or synchronicity will come from all around you. The Angels are very creative and will use whatever means necessary to communicate. It is our turned off inner knowing that keeps us from hearing clearly the Angles messages as they come.

17

The events and insights will be personalized just for you. The meanings of the things that are brought forth will be something that probably only you will understand. They more than likely will be quiet and subtle rather than dramatized as the movies portray things with lightning bolts and monstrous voices shouting out of the darkness. The Creator and his Messengers speak in whispers and love although they can be very dramatic if the situation warrants it.

Share your life and allow the glory, grace and joy of The Creator to come into your heart and bring you divine gifts and peace.

The answers and the journey are within. The still quiet moments within your own psyche with The Creator and The Creator's Messengers of hope and love are awaiting your invitation and acknowledgement. Listen for their whispers and feel the deep inner love that is only theirs to give. You have to but only open your hands to release your doubts, allow the Creator's love to wash over you, open to it, receive it, accept it and watch as you blossom and grow.

Peace be with you my Brothers and Sisters for we are all **ONE** *within The Creator's Spiritual Heart*

Perhaps you would like to write your own Angel Experiences Here? Journaling is a very important tool in the remembrance process.

ANGELS
By Carolyn Ann O'Riley

At the edge of dawn
The Angels wait.
Hoping for an invitation
To our inner state.

Peace they bring us,
Love Divine
Beauty and Wonder
Their hearts so kind.

God is waiting
His arms to enfold.
He whispers in our ear,
Of My love I have told.

We are rising to the moment
Our time is at hand.
The way is clearly marked.
United we stand.

Peace I give you,
Joy abounds,
Angels all around us,
Let our hearts feel the sounds.

Bliss and blessings, to us all.
Angels guide our way.
Heaven is above us,
They are expecting us today.

© From the Book " Go Within Feel The Love" By Carolyn Ann O'Riley

Chapter 2

<u>Author's Note</u>: The beginning Archangel Michael's Messages for public reading were for the students participating in the class "<u>A Course In I AM</u>". It was Archangel Michael's gift and support for the students as they strove to further their own spiritual expansion. Archangel Michael has requested that you read all of the messages that have come forth; therefore we have included the messages addressed to the participants of "<u>A Course In I AM</u>".

An Opening Message, For The Students of "A Course In I AM" From Archangel Michael

My beloved's, these materials were gathered with great care to offer to you tools, information, and exercises that will allow you to re-member who you really are.

Each is on a journey and each has individualized needs.

Share with all you know what you have learned within these classes and allow the love that is available to you now to permeate every part of your Beingness.

Take up your staff and begin your role as a leader and visionary within this Now for you are the way showers.

Allow this Messenger to over light each of you so that we may move forward with love and peace to a glorious New World where all is recognized as ONE again, pristine and within the Creator's Master Blueprint.

Show others the way and allow them their differences as they are allowing you your differences. Treat each Soul with kindness and remember that what you do to another you also are doing to yourselves, for we are all ONE within the Mind of The Creator.

And So It Is,
I Am Archangel Michael, The Creator's Messenger of Love, Joy, Wisdom, Light, Peace & Grace.

Write Your Angel Notes Here Do You Hear Them Speaking to you yet? Don't worry you will.

Chapter 3

Message For the Students of "A Course In I AM" From Archangel Michael

You are Divine Love manifested in physical form. You are beauty, you are grace, and you are whole and perfect just as you are. You are not your Body.

My beloveds don't confuse the body, which is illusion and only matter, with what you truly are.

You are so grand and this Messenger will help you remember. Listen to the material and feel the love as it searches you out and then lands in your heart center.

Feel this Messenger's presence for this Messenger is here with you always. Feel this Messenger's love for it is very real and cannot be denied even by those that are non-believers. Love conquers all things. You are love, we are all ONE. And so it is.

I Am Archangel Michael, The Creator's Messenger of Love, Joy, Wisdom, Light, Peace & Grace.

What Did Your Angels Whisper In Your Spiritual Ears?

Chapter 4

A Message From Archangel Michael

Beloveds, this is a time for examining all that is coming up in your lives to evaluate and clear all that old burned on stuff inside a cooking pot if you will. This class is about clearing and changing your perspectives of who you really are so that you can move forward on your paths with ease and grace.

Use the clearing tools within these class exercises daily and feel the differences within your physical bodily structure change and become lighter and lighter. Just image what is happening to your other bodies as this is occurring in the physical so it too is occurring all throughout your various levels, dimensions and aspects.

Change does require your daily intent and effort to become the entity that you truly are. Allow yourself this beautiful gift and work with the clearing energies to free yourselves of all this stuff that no longer serves your higher good.

Allow this Messenger to give you a gift, but one that you must actually ask me for in order to receive it. Those that ask, will receive four Angels that will be in addition to those you already have assigned. They are coming to you directly through this

Messenger's instructions. You may direct the Angels to assist you in your growth or whatever you feel you desire them to help with. Ask them their names, ask for their help and allow them to be there and love you.

This Messenger loves you most dearly my Warriors of Light

I Am Archangel Michael, The Creator's Messenger of Love, Joy, Wisdom, Light, Peace & Grace.

What Do You Remember ?

Chapter 5

Message From Archangel Michael For Class

Beautiful Beings Of Light, these are times of great change. Chaos is the norm rather than the occasional occurrence.

In times of such great change it is imperative that you ground yourself properly and clear as much from your various dimensions, levels and aspects in order to move through these time with Ease and Grace.

This Messenger asks you to begin integrating these exercises found in you lovingly prepared books in front of you, so that you might make the transition more smoothly with less physical symptoms and discomforts.

The more you clear the easier these changes will be.
The more you clear the more awareness will be coming within your path to embrace. The crystals that you have left as markers on your own path for reminders will be easier to find and recognize.

This Messenger is so proud of each of you for selecting to remember that you are grand Warriors of Light and are glowing beautiful beings beyond compare.

From the Heavens your lights are seen form the higher realms and they are growing in brilliance daily due to your efforts and hard work to remember who you really are.

This Messenger salutes you and will assist in your growth if asked.

This Messenger loves you each dearly

I Am Archangel Michael, The Creator's Messenger of Love, Joy, Wisdom, Light, Peace & Grace.

What Would You Like To Change Within You?

Chapter 6

A Message From Archangel Michael

My beloveds, your progress is wondrous to behold.
You are growing by leaps and bounds. Continue your path and allow your dreams to manifest as heart visions, this is the vision that you do not see with your physical eyes but with your heart.

Your heart vision will never lead you down a wrong path, but will only lead you into the light. This is the way of the prophets and the leaders. This is your destiny within this moment of NOW.

Ask yourself what you are bringing to share with all, that no one else has to offer. You are unique and cannot be duplicated.

What is your special gift? Ask for this Messenger's guidance and this Messenger will assist you in unfolding your mission on this Earth Plane.

This Messenger loves each and every one of you dearly.

I Am Archangel Michael, The Creator's Messenger of Love, Joy, Wisdom, Light, Peace & Grace.

What Needs To Be Released?

Chapter 7

<u>A Message From Archangel Michael</u>

Beloved Masters, the time of change is growing more and more intense. More than ever before you are being asked to walk in your integrity.

This Messenger asks that each of you center and ground yourselves daily. Begin talking with your higher self and learning to distinguish that voice that will be your guidance.

Trust what your higher self is showing you and remember that nothing is as it appears for this Earth Plane is but an illusion of Mass Consciousness. It is an agreement of your higher spiritual beings that have decided on how to define specific appearances and interpretations for learning and growth experiences that The Creator once desired.

The connection to the higher self has become so dim within the 3rd dimensional density among so many that The Creator is concerned about this dis-eased environment.

Resolve and release your core issues so that you may begin moving through these times with Ease and Grace, this is your gift if you will but ask for it and exercise it daily.

The spiritual path is a moment to moment journey something that is always present. To pick it up and put it away for the balance of the day is a disservice that you do not yet realize or understand, but you are getting there.

Be brave my Spiritual Warriors for you are loved beyond measure.

I Am Archangel Michael, The Creator's Messenger of Love, Joy, Wisdom, Light, Peace & Grace.

Your Angel Desire Is?

Chapter 8

<u>A Message From Archangel Michael</u>

Beloveds it is time to begin manifesting your dreams into your reality.

Dream as large as you can and see it in perfection. Imagine this Earth as a beautiful pristine place of peace and perfection. Sparkling, clean and glorious in all ways. Hold that thought for several minutes and know that you are working towards bringing that manifestation into the seeds of Mass Consciousness.

Now imagine yourself within this pristine glorious place. See yourself in peace and perfection.

Allow yourself the moments daily to envision this perfection. Put away your doubts and believe that it will be so and it will.

This Messenger loves you most dearly, My Children of Light.

I Am Archangel Michael, The Creator's Messenger of Love, Joy, Wisdom, Light, Peace & Grace.

Your Visions of Peace Is?

Chapter 9

<u>Message From Archangel Michael</u>

Beloved Beings of Light, you gather here to learn to sort out that which is your reality and that which is Mass Consciousness or others reality.

Within this learning process there are many curves and turns from which to select. Ask your four angels (that I have sent each one of you that have asked for this gift) to help you discern that which is yours to see and discern and that which belongs to another to own and be responsible for.

You probably are taking responsibility for things within this lifetime that really are another's lessons to learn. Have any of you found yourselves doing this?

Ask yourself and your Angels why you sense the need to take on another's burdens to carry. Ask yourself if you will, whether or not you have enough of your own weight and lessons to tie down your beautiful shining light body with such Earthly density.

How do you suppose that you can stop yourself from continuing along this self-defeating path of weighting yourselves down with others problems?

Ask for this Messenger's assistance if needed and this Messenger will bring the Mighty Blue Flaming Sword to sever the ties of all that bind and keep you bound to self-defeating behavior patterns.

This Messenger is here to assist and help you My Dearly Beloved Children of Light, but you must ask for the assistance.

This Messenger loves you most dearly

I Am Archangel Michael, The Creator's Messenger of Love, Joy, Wisdom, Light, Peace & Grace.

Write Down The Issues You Ask To Have Dissolved?

Chapter 10

<u>A Message From Archangel Michael</u>

Beloveds we have journeyed to this our final class, have we not.

What do you feel is the most important thing that you will take away from this class experience?

If nothing else comes into your mind perhaps that the most immediate thing that you can do if you need this Messenger's help is to ask for it.

This Messenger is here, if you will but ask.

Take away the limitations that you might place upon my response or the qualifications of how this Messenger can assist you and allow this Messenger to over light and guide you.

A time will come in the not too distant future when you will come to a fork in the road of your spiritual path and this Messenger asks that you call for assistance in that selection process.

Ask the Angels to daily assist you with your life and ask for their help in seeing that each moment comes, goes and is with ease and grace.

This Messenger loves you dearly My Loyal Light Workers.

I Am Archangel Michael, The Creator's Messenger of Love, Joy, Wisdom, Light, Peace & Grace.

Your Next Steps To Self Actualization Are?

First Love
By Carolyn Ann O'Riley

Twilight and Evening Hour
A Soft Kiss on the Lips.

Passion's warmth rushing through my body
Please don't stop, I felt so alive.

You're leaving!
Was that goodbye?

Or a delicious taste of
More days to come.

I'm new at this
Hold my hand.

Releasing.
By Carolyn Ann O'Riley

I release thee now anger
I release thee now might
I will follow my guidance
To do what I sense is right.

Leave me now pain
Leave me now fears
I embrace my own worthiness
No need to have tears.

Angels be by my side
Both day and night
Our Creator is calling
Come into the light.

The light will surround you
Protect you, enfold
Encircle your essence
In warm light and Gold.

Peace I leave you
Joy untold
Blessings have found you
Grace and love behold.

You are shinning
And beaming
Reflecting the light
Manifesting your dreams this glorious night.

You are Free

As We Are Called Home
By Carolyn Ann O'Riley

In the morning of peaceful silence
Comes God's voice from within my heart.
Telling me that all is well
And I will never again be left in the dark.

Oh! Those moments of pure bliss,
Dancing round the ballroom floor
Comes a knowledge deep inside
That I will be with the Creator forever more.

It won't be long now the Angels tell me
I'll be home in a blink of an eye
Oh the joy and acceleration
Coming home, entering that door.

All the warmth and love surrounding
As I enter God's peaceful gates
All my cries of home have vanished
I have started a brand new slate.

Peaceful now and filled with compassion
Looking down on those below
They will find their way without me
Of this I am certain and I know.

I leave them in God's love and presence
As they find their way back home
We will all be together shortly
As they heed the call, their journey done

Walk in silence
Feel the joy
Share the love
Forever more.

We Are One.

Chapter 11

<u>A Message From Archangel Michael,</u>

Beloved Masters, we have walked along now for quite some time, have we not.

The changes that are evolving are within The Creator's Divine Blueprint although many would say it is difficult to perceive why death and destruction might fit within that perfect plan.

The answer my Beautiful Beings of Light is that this is but an illusion where your egos have gotten the upper hand and you are being swept away in the currents of your ego's need for drama within your lives. Where you put your attention Beloveds is what will materialize within your physical planes of existence.

My Beautiful Beings if you are indeed tired of the dramas that continue to repeat and play themselves out, remember that all you need do is change your thoughts. If each person would change their thoughts the moment that a destructive thought or remembrance came into their minds then the destruction would cease.

Remind yourselves to not place your mind, thoughts and energies on that which you do not want. For it is you my Beloved Brothers and Sisters that are continuing to bring these episodes into the mass consciousness awareness and then they indeed are materialized within the 3D plane of existence.

Change the way you think and you will repeal this illusion that keeps you trapped and lacking in seeing that there is truly light and love at the end of the tunnel. The Creator is awaiting you with arms outstretched so to speak, to awaken from this nightmare of 3D desecration and remember who and what you really are.

The world can be changed one person at a time, but Dear Hearts that person is you and you are the only one that can make that change.

Remember that The Creator has only sent you Angels, Beautiful Beings of Light. There are no such things as demons and devils except of your own thoughts as dark devices and drama making episodes spurned from your ego to create your own fear.

This Messenger is Your Most Glorious Supporter OF Hope and Faith That You Will Remember From Whence You Came and Who You Really Are.

Be at Peace and Know that All Is Within The Divine Blue Print Of The Creator, All Is In Perfection.

You Are Loved By The Creator beyond Earthly measure, re-member that Love. Allow it to lead you on the path Home

I Am Archangel Michael, The Creator's Messenger of Love, Joy, Wisdom, Light, Peace & Grace.

How did Archangel Michael's message make you feel?

Chapter 12

A Message From Archangel Michael

Greetings Beloved Beings of Light, in the United States this is a weekend of celebration of independence from oppressive governments of the past and Freedom of persons to choose the way in which they want to live.

My Wondrous Warriors, each day is a day of celebration of choice for each of you moment by moment choose exactly what it is that you will do and that which you will not do.

Your acceptance of this responsibility within your Beingness is one way of moving further up on your spiritual path, so to speak. What a glorious opportunity and gift this is a moment at a time to choose each action, word, thought, and so forth that comes and graces your lives.

When one acknowledges with intent that they realize that they are accepting the responsibility of each moment of their lives the veil begins to crumble further and further as you understand and accept that you are not these bodies and this is but an exercise of lessons in the School within The Earth Plane.

You then understand that you have pre-chosen all that is coming into your lives and that you are then capable of the next step and that is beginning to comprehend that you also control your thoughts that create within this material particle environment. The responsibility of your presence then begins to really press upon your shoulders as you begin to perceive that you are creating what is happening around you. For you see that you have the choice and the power to change that which you create with your thoughts.

My glorious Light Beings begin to come to grips with your ability to draw forth energy to create and understand that your thoughts are creating the future of mass consciousness.

Your mission here on this Earth Plane at this time is to dissolve old stuck out dated thinking processes. Release all the old paradigms, and past programming and begin to replace this out dated pattern with that of the glorious pristine image and vision of The Creator's Master Blue Print of perfection.

Ask for assistance and guidance to help you understand further your individual mission upon the Planet and Ask for The Creator's guidance in helping your discern what your next steps should be.

Go deep within yourselves and begin the process of generating that pristine vision that is to replace this destruction and desecration of Mother Earth at all levels.

The mission is yours my Light Warriors and this Messenger can see your potential and know that this is accomplishable.

Your lights are shinning brighter and brighter and your glowing presence is illuminating the heavens so brightly. The Creator is so proud of each and every one of His/hers Children.

I Am Archangel Michael, The Creator's Messenger of Love, Joy, Wisdom, Light, Peace & Grace.

What notes would you like to make about your visualization, date them and put them away to revisit at a later time.

Chapter 13

A Message From Archangel Michael
Intent & Relationships

Beloved Warriors of Light tonight I come to speak to you about intent and relationships.

Humanity has changed so since the first breaths were taken in physicality. Fascinations of all types both wondrous and not so glorious have become common place.

The stress and chaos caused by material requirements is something that we shall look at tonight and work with, you and I. I want you to begin looking at relationships and begin the evaluation of what they mean in your everyday lives and with those you state you love.

What has man/woman/child gained by having things if they alienate the soul and those we are wanting to draw near us with love? But perhaps the question should be what is the worth of a relationship on whatever level that might be between whatever entities or animal that might be.

There is a definite relationship whether perceived and understood between your need for things and your relationships at all levels.

Beautiful Beings of Light, let's take the relationship of a pet just as an example to demonstrate and question the depth of our true love and intention in having a pet.

Most pets within a family environment on the Earth Plane hold a high position of respect and love from all within the family unit.

Some sad to say even hold more respect and awe than those humans within the family unite. Look at the relationship closely. Take it apart and really come to terms with your depth of sharing love with this animal family member.

The pet is obtained to add love or companionship to the family unit. Ask the following questions: Was the intention for bring in the pet, based at the highest level in consideration of the pet's needs for companionship, attention, care, health maintenance and so forth, or was the pet brought in to add love to the family without regard to the pet's own needs.

If the situation is like most family unites today the pet is brought in to a two person working environment or a single parent home perhaps with children maybe without children. Even if one parent doesn't work the same will hold true as an example. The pet has probably been left alone for extended lengths of time either because no one is home or is ignored due to activity overload. Generally the parents or care givers comes home from their jobs stressed and drained of all passion for themselves, their children, their pets let alone any desire to complete the self-required chores and family maintenance or activity schedules. So much is involved in truly caring for each family member, the material requirements of each family member, the general care and feeding of a family member, their personal growth paths and on and on.

So let's ask while looking at it from this stand point what was served here by bringing in a pet? Was the pet served by bring in additional love or has the pet added to the stress due to the requirements of its maintenance alongside the needs and the balance of the family member's needs. Was the amount of time given to the pet in love and attention worthy of the love that the pet unconditionally returns to the owners or care givers?

Each relationship needs to be viewed in the very same way for all desire the very highest level of unconditional love that is appropriate for them each moment within this Earth Plane life time.

Do you sense that this perhaps is how the feelings of lack and un-love have been created within each being?

By entering into a relationship whether it is an employment relationship, friend, family, love relationship, pet relationship or whatever, are your eyes and your hearts wide open with truth and wisdom to show exactly what it is that you are indeed seeking and willing to share and give within that relationship?

Dig deep here and be truthful with yourself.

Are you willing to give the relationship the moments and love that each require? What feelings do you think this creates when the highest of intentions is not given to the interaction.

Has materialism become so ingrained that the trait of requiring more and more things has now been transferred on to humans and pets as the need to continue to add more and more relationships whether or not the quality of the relationship and moments shared equaled the commitment.

What are the intentions within each of your lives regarding those that you have chosen to interact and become part of their core interaction group?

Are mates being given the amount of attention and unconditional love that each deserves? Are children being given the amount of attention and unconditional love that each deserves.

Was the child's entry into the family unite considered and calculated because there was available time to completely fill each child's love and attention requirements after all other relationship quotas of love and attention were completed. After their arrival whether planned or not, they were greeted with the unconditional love that The Creator showered upon them prior to their re-emergence upon Earth.

Is the work environment being reviewed for its ability to allow one to go home and fulfill their family's love and attention needs? Is the work place requiring more than is worthy of its role to meet the financial needs of the material chosen requirements that humans have decided are required for their happiness?

Do you question how much is enough materially and then begin to downsize to fit the new criteria of what is really important within your life?

Would it be worth considering what each relationship means and whether it's needs have been meet. If analyzed and found wanting are you willing to release the relationship with unconditional love so that their highest good can be served.

In those relationships that cannot be released such as a child can you then understand their anger and lack that lurks there and begin to see that this is what needs mending.

These times are about releasing all that no longer serve, but first understanding of what is involved and how it interacts and effects is needed to correctly evaluate what is happening.

Yes contracts have been created prior to entry onto this Earth Plane, but also The Creator's Master Blueprint of Change is upon this glorious beautiful planet.

A time of reckoning is here and interactions, intent and relationships are key components to bring about The Creator's Master Plans of Perfection.

This Messenger brings you these questions to ponder and ask yourself what is your intent, and how has each relationship been served?

Ask yourself what higher good of your own and others has been served by requiring yourself to work harder and harder to obtain things versus bring understanding, attention and unconditional love to yourself and those that are closest and most dear to you. Look even higher and ask and allow The Creator to fill you heart to over flowing so that you will have so much more unconditional love to share.

This Messenger loves you most dearly my Warriors of Light and I bring you these queries, allow them to seep into your hearts and begin to open your inner eyes so that you bring in the love that you truly deserve.

This Messenger is here Beloveds should you ask for help.

I Am Archangel Michael, The Creator's Messenger of Love, Joy, Wisdom, Light, Peace & Grace.

Your Relationship Intentions Reviewed Here

Chapter 14

A Message from Archangel Michael

The Self Image

Beloveds, the message that I deliver today regards your self-image.

To love another one must first love self.

How do you see yourself?

What is the criterion that you see within and without to give yourself the accurate picture of who you see yourself to be?

Are others used as the mirror to determine what that image is or do you go within to get in touch with that knowing spirit that tells you what and who you really are? Do you then take that inner truth of beauty and know that the physical is but a small part of the real you and not allow others to dampen that knowing or change that vision by projecting their pictures of what is acceptable in their 3D physical world, not yours?

Do you see yourself only with a physical body? Do you see yourself with parts of that physical vessel that you don't necessarily like? Ever just feel like climbing out of your skin?

Do you then ponder about that physical body and obsess that for example your nose is too big or your thighs are not slender or you are not tall enough or that your stomach is to large or there is some deformity or abnormality that you have selected prior to your incarnation that you have allowed to dampen your inner perfection and beauty. Are these thoughts familiar to you my Beautiful Warriors of Light?

Are you remembering how easy shedding of the physical body can be? Do you sense that leaving this physical vessel behind might be what those dissatisfactions are about?

How can anything that is made in the Creator's perfection have flaws? Have you ever wondered how such a magnificent image has become so distorted over time that we find flaws and imperfections within the Creator's handy work?

That glorious light being that is you is only temporarily playing a physical part, remind yourself of this Beloveds. That physical form is yours to change to your own satisfaction in whatever way is most pleasing to you my Glorious Beings of Light.

Your hair is yours to change, your weight is yours to change, all of these things and more are strictly physical attributes of your own making.

Do you sense that your physical body is loved and cherished for its beauty in whatever way and perfection that it is in, or do you criticized it and treat it with lack of respect because there is something about it that you do not like? Where do you think that dislike and dissatisfaction has stemmed from? Do you ever watch movies, television or read magazines? Do you believe there is a connection there of some type? Why would you allow a media image to make you feel less than beautiful? When one understands that each is a masterpiece of perfection that cannot be duplicated by another, why would you compare one miracle with another? There is no competition within The Creator's mind between The Creator's children.

How can you learn to love your physical body? Oh my Beloveds by seeing it in the perfection that it truly is and in total harmony and balance within your own energies fields. There is nothing there that you have not selected or chosen. It is of your making. See it as perfect in whatever way it is. Love it as perfect without flaw and see what happens to your self-esteem. Accept that you are indeed a Beautiful Being of Light and that you are in perfection as we speak, simply playing a physical role on this Earth Plane.

Feel my love and that of The Creator for we see you only in the perfection that you were created in and we love you however you are.

We love you most profoundly,

Peace be with you my Shinning Warriors you are needed here to bring Heaven to Earth, be happy in your physical forms for you have not been forgotten or forsaken, you are indeed in The Creator's Master Blueprint of Perfection.

I Am Archangel Michael, The Creator's Messenger of Love, Joy, Wisdom, Light, Peace & Grace.

Notes you would like to make relative to yourself image.

Chapter 15
<u>A Message From Archangel Michael</u>

<u>Catalysts</u>

Beloved Masters much is going on in your 3D world that you do not understand or perceive why it is happening.

It physically appears to human eyes as chaos, death, destruction, suffering and indifference, intolerance, anger and fear.

I tell you Beautiful Beings of Light that it is all within the Creator's Master Blue Print and is within The Creator's Perfection.

These are areas that are coming up to be reviewed and cleared, and released back into the energy of the Omniverse so that the energies of those outdated programs, relationships and all things that no longer serve can be re-qualified into the purest of perfections once again.

Try to visualize it Dearly Beloveds as a pot being brought to boil and then allowed to continue boiling to remove the cooked on debris that has been accumulating for thousands of years.

With each vibration rise and magnificent rays of the purest and highest love and glorious energies permeating the planet the pot will continue to boil over until all is pristine and aligned with the <u>One</u> again. Issues for you individually will continue to surface as well as with the whole until all are cleared and released. Ask for assistance from your Angels. Ask that they help to assist you so that each moment can be experienced with ease and grace instead of struggle and fear. They are but awaiting your invitation. Allow them to love and help you.

Many are leaving the planet Dear Ones as they decided at this time in now to do, prior to their entry into this incarnation. They bravely volunteered my Masters to experience these times and participate within these dramas that you are reading about and viewing on your news channels. This is their gift to humanity. They wished to participate to help clear old energies and allow their departure to bring unity back to the One. Their deaths are not forgotten and are catalysts to reunify all those that have awaken and hear the call to clear what is no longer serving the All.

Beloveds they agreed to these events and acts, they are not victims or villains. These are indeed brave souls and they are held in such high esteem within the Heavenly Hierarchy for their participation in this very special time of transition within the Earth Plane This is a planet of Free Will and these are occurrences that you have chosen. You've made these decisions on a higher level and then veiled yourself from your remembrances.

We greet those returning, my Beautiful Beings of Light, with so much love and celebration for this is indeed their time to travel higher on the spiral of their growth and evolution.

They will be missed on the Earth Plane but know and see them within their eternal existence for that is the case my Warriors of Light. Each of you is an eternal Beautiful Being of Light. You are not the physical flesh that you see with your physical eyes when you view yourself in the earthly mirror. Look deeper within your eyes and begin to see yourselves as the Beings of Light that are all ways an eternal fragment of The Creator.

This is a blessed time of growth and change. Change to many is very uncomfortable. To some it is fearful for they only see with their physical eyes the dramas that are unfolding within their physical surroundings. All is not as it seems Brave Warriors. Go Deeper Within.

When you pray to The Creator place this question to The Creator to answer for you: What would you have me know?
Expect and answer and allow that answer to manifest in whatever way is appropriate for you. Thank the Creator for the answer for my Beloveds it will indeed be answered.

My Beloveds a need to go deeper within is very much what we would recommend for these times that are so difficult to watch. Your peace will be found within. This will be your solace and blessed serenity, from that which is happening all around you.

I offer this meditation to you as a gift to bring you closer to The Creator and closer to your spiritual families, guides, angels and all Heavenly Hierarchy that are surrounding you with their love and devotion. You are so dearly loved. There is not a one of you that is alone. Your veil has just not lifted so that you can spiritually see their presence. Ask for this to be so. Ask for the veil to be removed and ask for greater understanding of what is happening so that you can make peace within your heart and move forward within your own grow and awakening.

Ask for my help Beloveds ask for the inner peace that I will gladly share with you.

Your Meditation:
This Messenger asks that you find a quiet place that you will not be disturbed for 15 minutes or so.
You may sit or lay down, as you prefer. Get very comfortable and if you wish lay a small cover over you so that you will not be

distracted should your body become cool while it is being relaxed and calmed during this meditation.

Close your beautiful eyes. Take three sets of very deep cleansings breaths. Upon the last deep breath upon the exhale just let it flow out in a sight.

I ask that you ask your subconscious mind to step aside and perch on your left shoulder during this meditation. Invite and allow your Higher Self to fully come within and take over this process and integration within this time frame.

Visualize with your Spiritual Eyes The Creator sending down a glorious white protective beam of light. It is traveling down from the corner of the ceiling into your crown chakra and permeating all your Beingness. It is completely filling your Beingness with white light and now is expanding out through your finger tips and permeating all that is within the room, now traveling out further and completely permeating all within the building that you are in. You are now Divinely protected and only those things that are for your highest good can even communicate with you. You are the only one that can give permission for anything that is not for your highest good to communicate with you in any way during this time.

Let's journey together now you and I. I do ask if I have your permission to travel with you on this trip as I too must have your permission and be extended an invitation to accompany you. If it is right for you then I accept the invitation and the journey begins. Ask your other Guides and Angels to join you if you so desire.

Visualize yourself traveling to a crystal palace deep within your heart's center. In your mind's eye you are creating your own individualized visualization so as I describe things along your path allow your own interpretations to guide the appearance and surroundings to exactly the way you desire to see them. You are breathing very evenly now and feel secure and safe. This inner space is a very private place and only those that you invite may enter. See a door in front of you and you turn the handle and step through the thresh hole. You are entering a lush green meadow with a brook running alongside with a bank of tall beautiful trees. You can hear the wind whispering to you through the tree branches saying, "Welcome, Welcome back". Listen to the brook as the water giggles rolling over the small smooth pebbles and stones as you walk beside it on the path to the bridge. The brook is gurgling, "Welcome, we love you" and you hear it saying, "it has been to long since we've seen you". The bridge is in front of you, it crosses the brook and is made of wood and is arched in the center. Upon reaching the other side you can feel a definite shift of consciousness as you are reaching another milestone on this journey. You see in front of you a mountain with steps up the side. As you approach the steps I ask that each of you remove and leave your backpacks at the base of the steps that are filled with problems frustrations, doubts, lack, judgment of others, self-judgment, feelings of unworthiness and shame. You can pick them back up again on your return if you so choose to do so, but for now leave them there.

Oh! Feel how good that feels to have that weight taken off of your shoulders. It is so freeing. You begin the ascent up the steps and as you climb to the next higher step you are feeling lighter and lighter.

You are reaching the top and see that you are in your Garden of Serenity. You are creating this garden within your mind exactly as you desire to see it. You linger only a moment longer as you know that you can return here anytime you choose, now that you have remembered the way.

Walking through the garden speaking and smiling to all the plants, trees, and various creatures within your garden. You see in front of you a large crystal palace, sparkling in the light. It glows and feels so warm and loving just to look at it. At the entry there are two white marble columns with your birth dates inscribed on each one. Between the columns is the palace doorway. As you look closer you see the door is solid gold. A closer look still and you see your name as it was gifted to you at the time of your creation. What does it say? Underneath that name there are other names that you have assumed throughout your many past existences. Some may be in languages that you do not understand or markings that you do not recognize. You look down the list and see your present name engraved on the door. Do not be concerned if you do not see any other names but the one that you presently hold. This information is not ready for you yet and it will come forth when the moment is appropriate.

You turn the handle on the golden door and step inside. It looks however you desire to see it. It is beautiful beyond compare filled with all the gifts and wealth that are yours to hold and the light is filtering into the inner area from all the facets of the crystal construction material refracting all the wondrous colors of the rainbow. You can walk and stand in each color if you like. Feel the differences between each color as each carries its own energies and attributes. You will know just the right one to stand in at this moment. That knowing is all coming back to you now.

You notice that there are many many doors inside this palace each is labeled but you might not be able to read the signs on each door yet. The door closest to you how ever has light emanating from all around it and under it. You can feel a presence behind the door like no other. You walk closer and the sign on the door says The Creator. One of the door signs says My Angles, another Ascended Masters, another Spiritual Family, another Guides, another Spirit Physicians and many many more.

This journey however you are going to visit your pool of Christ Consciousness. You make your way to the center of the palace and see an enclosed pool with a vapor of rainbow hues rising above the water there. You step through the thresh hold and remove your shoes.

All of those that you have invited and your Angels are with you and I, Archangel Michael am there seated next to the pool awaiting your arrival. Archangel Gabriel, Uriel, Raphael, and Zadkiel are here as well, all seated in different locations around the edge of the pool. The beautiful vapors almost have them completely concealed but you can feel their love emanating to you and you know they are with you on this most precious occasion.

The Angels motion for you to step in a circle area with a low silver violet flame. As you stand within that area the flame permeate all parts of your Beingness changing color from silver violet to white. The flames are cool and soothing and you have no fear of them because they do not burn the skin they are clearing and purifying all levels, dimensions and aspects of your Beingness.

The Angels next motion for you to step into the pool allowing the rainbow hued vapors to enfold and engulf you. The water is refreshing. You sense that your body is becoming more transparent and luminous. You are now noticing as the veil thins and your heart begins to focus clearly the colors of all your different bodies. You appear with all of your colors as perhaps a beautiful translucent butterfly would appear. Your size is expanded with all the different colored layers that are the real you.

Through the misty vapors you are perceiving a figure approaching. As you adjust your spiritual heart eyes and focus more clearly you see the figure coming closer and closer. It is beaming brilliantly and as it now stands before you, the light is so bright you cannot look directly into it.

The Being is the Christ Consciousness. It takes its hand and removes a piece of its own heart and motions for you to come closer. The Being then places this golden solar heart piece within

83

your own Heart Chakra. It instantly expands to fill that space in just the right proportions.

You are instantly filled with so much love, you feel as though you can hold no more and may burst with so much love. The Being then instructs you to share this heart with all you desire to gift, especially the little babies coming into this Earth Plane. It tells you that the more you share of this Solar Heart the more will be returned and the stronger this Solar Heart will become.

The Being backs into the mist and disappears but the feeling of love lingers and will never leave you. You have received a piece of home and a remembrance of what it feels like again.

I along with Archangel Gabriel, Uriel, Raphael and Zadkiel, gather around you and place our spiritual hands over your heart and add our energies to this wonderful gift.

The Angels lead you out of the pool and you once again begin to retain your physical vessel form although now more faint in mass clarity. It will never be the same again. You have given intent to allow yourself to journey further upon this path.

You open the door of the enclosed garden and walk to the door marked The Creator. The brilliant light burst forth and is almost blinding. You hear a voice that is so familiar to you now, the voice of The Creator says to you " Come in My Child I have Been Waiting for your Visit" "I love you so dearly" "There is no other like you for I only create perfection and you are part of that which is perfect." The Creator motions to you to take Its hand. You feel an energy surge like you have never experienced before on this Earth Plane. The Creator asks you to dance and you move into the traditional ballroom dance positions and you feel the music as your spiritual hand touches The Creator's magnificence and you begin slowly whirling into a waltz around the room with the Creator. You move with such fluid grace and ease, you have never been guided and danced so magnificently before. You are filled with such wonder and aw. As you are whirling on the dance floor you merge into the One Essence that is The Creator. You sense no beginning and no end. You expand and become as large as the universe. You are All and All is you.

You sense it is time to return to your physical realm once more and begin to slowly stop twirling and disengage from The Creator. Saddened to do so but The Creator reminds you that you have much work to do. Your missions here are not yet over and it is time to return. You may retain your memories of this experience to remind you that you are loved beyond measure and this is the true feeling of Love that you have so longingly searched for within your physical live times. The feeling of Oneness with The All That Is.

You give The Creator one final hug and turn and go out The Creator's door, gliding back into the palace and through the thresh hold door. Back down the path in the Garden of Serenity back down the mountain side steps, deciding not to pick the backpacks back up again at the bottom of the steps. You cross back over the bridge and back up the path back through your heart chakra door and back into this physical reality.

Wiggle your fingers and your toes you are returning to your physical vessels once more to fulfill your destinies.

My Beloveds I give you this meditation gift and ask you to use it frequently. It will assist in calming your fears and strengthen that which needs balance and harmony within your physical world to continue your mission within this Earth Plane.

I Am Archangel Michael, The Creator's Messenger of Love, Joy, Wisdom, Light, Peace & Grace.

Write Down Your Experiences During This Meditation

Chapter 16

A Message From Archangel Michael

Allow The Healing and Releasing to Enfold You

The time is now my Beautiful Masters. The inner work is beckoning to place you on the path to which you are being called.

Look deep within your hearts and take inventory of those things that no longer serve your highest good?

Look deep within all layers, within all charkas, within all levels, dimensions and aspects. Give your Angels permission to help you bring these things into your awareness. It is only within your awareness and with your permission that these things can be released.

Be brave my Beautiful Beings Of Light for some of you are carrying a great deal buried within that may appear to be dark and verboten. Please understand that Darkness is just the opposite polarity of light and devoid of all light.

Those things that have been created by your constant thoughts, worry, anxieties, and fears can materialize as all types of shadow selves that are mistaken for very dark forms. Remember that which you place your attention, thoughts and energies on will materialize. You My Beloved Warriors are Creators do you remember? Please Beloved Warriors, do not place your attention and energy on those things that you do not want within your realities for they will be come into being.

All levels dimensions and aspects of you that you are, must be cleared of all old energies, patterns, programs, relationships, angers, fears, and negative thought forms.

Each time your release pieces of these parts that no longer serve your highest good you become lighter and lighter. This allows you to stop repeating over and over the lessons that occurred from these past portions of your old outdated selves.

Here is an exercise that will begin to put things into perspective for you, repeat this exercise three times each session, perform three times per day. This is something that you can do anywhere no one need even be aware that you are doing this:

Repeat to yourself: " I Am Only Placing My Attention On Those Things that I Am Manifesting Within Myself Now"

" I Am Only Placing My Attention On Those Things that I Am Manifesting Within Myself Now"

" I Am Only Placing My Attention On Those Things that I Am Manifesting Within Myself Now"

This Messenger gifts you with another meditation that will assist in this practice for your use. Work with it for the next 30 days and feel the progress as you allow yourself to lighten your load on this Earth Plane.

A note about Meditation my Beloved Light Warriors, if you record these meditations and while listening you fall asleep do not be concerned, you are still obtaining the benefit because, they are being utilized by other levels and dimensions of your Beingness.

Also as description and visualization comes forth, allow your own Being to perceive this in any way that is appropriate. Limitation has no place within the Universe. You will create that which you need to sense or visualize. Know that if information does not flow or come forth as described that it is not time for you to have the information, it will come when appropriate within The Creator's Time Frame.

Know that if you ask for my presence my Beautiful Beings Of Light That I Am with you. Release the doubt, I Am there.

Many times within the physical Beingness one cannot talk face to face with the individual that is most needed to communicate with, for whatever reason or even out of fear. And let's say that if the Beingness could communicate, the physical body that would be present would not allow the communication to take place for whatever reason, be it selective listening, violence, abuse, addictions, or even their death or transformation to another plane of that entity's existence. All issues can be discussed with their Higher Self My Beautiful Beings of Light, even if the other individual has departed the Earth Plane. This is a meditative tool to allow each Beingness to begin working through those issues of impacted energy that are keeping you stuck.

With your permission, this Messenger is taking you on a journey of Healing and Releasing. This is a journey you have made many times before, but perhaps just do not remember.

Find a quiet spot where you will not be disturbed for 30 minutes or so. Sit or lie down if you like with your eyes closed in whatever is the most comfortable position for you. Clear your mind of all thoughts. Begin by taking three deep breaths, fully inhaling and exhaling. Begin relaxing all parts of your body individually as you continue to take deep breaths in and out. Allow your body to begin feeling that delightful light feeling of settling into serenity and peace. The next breath in and just allow the breath out as you exhale this time allow this breath to come out as a sigh.

Thank The Creator for this beautiful gift of healing and releasing. Invite your Angels, Guides, Ascended Masters and Spiritual Family to join you on this journey. The Creator is sending down a beautiful protective beam of white light and it is coming down from the corner of the room where you are meditating. It is entering through your crown chakra and permeating all parts of your Beingness and it is now radiating and emanating out from your bodies, filling and permeating all parts of the room that you are occupying. You are now protected and enfolded in The Creator's Love.

You are traveling to your crystal palace deep within your heart center, you are breathing very evenly now and feel secure and safe. This inner space is a very private place and only those that you invite may enter. See a door in front of you and you turn the handle and step through the thresh hole. See that it enters a meadow with a brook running alongside the bank, see the tall beautiful trees. Listen to the brook as the water giggles rolling over the small smooth pebbles. It is saying welcome Beautiful Being and that it loves you and it has been a long time since it's seen your presence here. A wooden bridge arched in the center is in front of you, it crosses the brook. You reach the other side and feel a definite shift of reality as if you have reached another milestone in your journey. See in front of you a mountain with steps up the side. As you approach the steps remove and leave your backpacks filled with your problems and frustrations at the base of the steps. You may pick them back up again on you return if you so choose, but for now leave them there.

Oh! Feel how good that feels to have that weight taken off of your shoulders. It is so freeing. Begin the ascent up the steps and as you climb to the next higher step you are feeling lighter and lighter.

Upon reaching the top, see that you are in your garden of serenity. You are creating this garden within your mind's eye. It can look anyway that you wish it to look. Does it have trees or plants perhaps and what about grass or water falls. Does your garden have animals and what do they look like. Linger only a moment longer as you know you can return here anytime you choose, now that you have remembered the way.

Walking through the garden you see in front of you a large crystal palace, sparkling in the light. It glows and feels so warm and loving just to look at it. At the entry there are two white marble columns with your birth dates inscribed on each one. Between the columns is the palace doorway. As you look closer you see the door is solid gold. A closer look still and you see your name as it was gifted to you at the time of your creation. What does it say? Underneath that name there are other names that you have assumed throughout your many past existences. Some may be in languages that you do not understand or markings that you do not recognize. You look down the list and see your present name engraved on the door as well. Do not be concerned if you do not see any other names but the one that you presently hold. For this information is not ready for you yet and it will come forth when the moment is appropriate.

You turn the handle on the golden door and step inside. It looks however you desire to see it. It is beautiful beyond compare filled with all the gifts and wealth that are yours to hold. The light is filtering into the inner area from all the facets of the crystal construction material refracting all the wondrous colors of the rainbow. You can walk and stand in each color if you like. Feel the differences between each color as each carries its own energies and attributes. You will know just the right one to stand in and when. Hear each color whisper it's special message to you. That knowing is all coming back to you now.

You notice that there are many many doors inside this palace each is labeled but you might not be able to read the signs on each door yet. The door closest to you however has light emanating from all around it and under it. You can feel a presence behind the door like no other. You walk closer and the sign on the door says The Creator. One of the door signs says my Angles, another Ascended Masters, another spiritual family, another spirit physicians. There are many more doors, but you know where you are going now. This seems very familiar and you are walking down a hall and standing in front of the door that says " Healing and Releasing Room".

You enter this room and as before you make it as beautiful as you can. Fill it full of all the conveniences you think you will desire as you will be spending a great deal of time here. You might find a pool within this room. You might want to label it the Healing Pool. Perhaps this pool has healing soothing emerald green water and it could have lotus blossoms floating on the surface if you like. It looks so inviting, but you remember why you are here. You remember that you are here to call on the higher selves of one or those that you have some relationship issues with or maybe have had a disagreement, an abuse issue, work issue or maybe just don't understand them or their behavior.

You ask for all those entities that you are comfortable inviting to come through their doors at this time and join you for support and comfort as you begin. Ask For My Presence if that is comfortable for you. My Blue Flaming Sword will come forth as well. You are well supported now feel our presences. You call the one within your mind to come before you now. Greet the invited one. Thank them for coming. Tell this person's higher self within your mind, you are communicating with them via mental telepathy, what it is that has been bothering you about the relationship or whatever you might need to discuss. Some time is available here for this communication.

You sense that you have communicated all that you want to communicate for this first session. They may return if invited again and again until all issues have been resolved. Closing the conversation thank them for coming again tell them that you thank them for the lessons that they have taught you, but you no longer have a need for those lesson in your life, you have learned the lessons well and have no need to constantly repeat them over and over again. The Mighty Blue Flaming Sword will sever the cords that bind you to each other. See the cords fall to the floor and instantly disappear. Feel how wondrous this feels not to be tied to this individual in this way any longer. Tell the other higher self that they may go and see them leave through the healing door out into the Universe. The door is now closed and securely fastened.

You might be feeling a little drained and tired at this moment having worked through and having released a major relationship issue or even shed a few tears. Allow yourself the glorious privilege of taking off whatever you might be wearing and just slip into the healing pool, feeling that luscious warm and inviting emerald green water slide over your body as you walk down the descending pool steps. If you like, invite those you asked for support to join you, ask Archangel Uriel, Gabriel and Raphael to join you allow them to surround your pool and beam their healing and loving energies into your pool to help you re-energize and revitalize.

You are feeling much better now, refreshed and are ready to return to your reality. You step out of the pool and dry off putting on whatever you want to wear and walk back up the hall and out into the Serenity Garden. You look back and know that you can return at any time for you have remembered the way.

You walk back down the steps of the mountainside. If you must you may pick up the backpack filled with problems and issues that you left. Ask yourself before putting them back on, did you really miss their presence and the stress that they presented in your life. If you choose to put the backpack on again, notice the tremendous weight that you have once again saddled yourself with.

Cross back over the bridge and back into your own being wiggling your fingers and your toes and when you are ready open your eyes and stir around.

How do you feel? Were you there?

This Messenger loves you most profoundly my Beautiful Beings of Light.

I Am Archangel Michael, The Creator's Messenger of Love, Joy, Wisdom, Light, Peace & Grace.

Your Meditation Experiences, What Spoke To Your Soul?

Chapter 17

A Message From Archangel Michael

A Rainbow Walk

Beloved Beautiful Beings of Light today's message carries forward the continued need to practice and work with releasing all that no longer resonates for your highest good and the good of all concerned.

The past messages have carried releasing exercises and meditations. My Warriors some may in fact sound repetitious, but the clearing and healing that has been wrought from these practices is worthy of all the efforts.

Your beacon lights are shinning so brightly now that the debris is being transmuted and released from your energy fields. The heavens are blazing and the vibrations are growing higher and higher. We are so very proud of you for your work and intent in working towards your next steps.

It takes courage to go forward and it is reflected within your efforts and the results are apparent from our vantage point. What were once gray clogged outer bodies are become brighter and brighter bodies of wondrous colors. Clearer more defined hues are surfacing. Your badges of honor are showing my Beloveds. The tarnish is being removed by the silver polish if you will.

Your veils are thinning. Do you not feel the difference within yourselves? Take a moment and allow that wondrous recognition to occur. Your lives may have been going in such a feverish pitch that you have not noticed the difference that is occurring within your own biology due to your work.

Do you not find yourself to be more cognizant of the very beauty of nature that is around you? Have you found yourself humming at the most unusual times? Have you noticed that spring in your step and that glorious smile coming back to your face when you greet another?

Connect the effort you have put forth with this change and allow yourself to be hugged by The Creator. Feel that love rush that is emanating from The Creator as it washes over you. Remind you of Home? Remind you of the Spiritual Family you left behind when you incarnated? Feel the love pouring out from you now and filling up all that you come in contact with. Allow yourself to visualize that love filling up all and continuing to grow and expand further and further out past the confines of the Earth and out into The Universe. Then sense that The Universe is sending it back to you again reinforced with even more intense Pink Love Light this time. Such joy and bliss is yours my Beautiful Beings of Light you are so very worthy of it. Allow yourself to sense it and feel it and accept it as so.

This evening another gift coming forth for you in the form of a new meditation. We will call this the Journey of Release Across the Rainbow Bridge.

Beloveds each judgment that is made, each responsibility that is assumed from someone else, each promise made, each relationship entered into, binds each to the other with cords of expectations, approvals, judgments, promises, commitments, conditions, etc. If you could see from our vantage point, you would see that most all are bound so tightly with cords that you look like mummies, so to speak wrapped so tightly with all the cords that bind one to another for whatever reason. This is an accumulation from your present lifetime and all those previous life times. This is causing the feeling of being stuck for you literally because you are all most so covered that you cannot move freely. This meditation severs the cords and allows you to release and free yourself of all those stuck energies that no longer serve your highest good.

You may repeat this exercise as often as you like.

Find a quiet spot where you will not be disturbed for 30 minutes or so. Sit or lie down if you like with your eyes closed in whatever is the most comfortable position for you. Clear your mind of all thoughts. Begin by taking three deep breaths, fully inhaling and exhaling. Begin relaxing all parts of your body individually as you continue to take deep breaths in and out. Allow your body to begin feeling that delightful light feeling of settling into serenity and peace. The next breath in and just allow the breath out as you exhale to come out as a sigh.

Thank The Creator for this beautiful gift of releasing and this message of love that The Creator has had me deliver to you. Invite your Angels, Guides, Ascended Masters and Spiritual Family to join you on this journey. With your permission I will join you as well. Ask The Creator to send a beautiful protective beam of white light and see it coming down from the corner of the room where you are meditating. It is entering through your crown chakras and permeating all parts of your Beingness and it is now radiating and emanating out from your bodies, filling and permeating all parts of the room that you are occupying. You are now protected and enfolded in The Creator's Love. Nothing can disturb you here without your permission.

If for some reason this is not resonating with you just put it aside. It is not your time to work with this material yet, but for those that are ready let's continue.

Ask your conscious mind to step aside. For this journey, ask your conscious mind to sit and be the observer on your left shoulder. Ask your Higher Self, the true you that is you, to merge and integrate within your Beingness. Now see your energies coming up from your root chakra all the way up the charka system and exiting out through your third eye, visualize the you that is really you, re-entering your heart chakra. See through your heart eyes yourself walking down as you descend the stairwell within the heart chakra. Through your closed eyes you are visualizing a doorway with the light emanating from around it and a sign that says "To The Rainbow Bridge". You turn the handle of the door and step across the threshold on to a puffy pure white cloud. You find that you can bounce up and down on the cloud and that it laughs with you as you sense the joy of innocent childhood play by bouncing up and down as if it were your bed at home.

Your adventure is now starting and you gather yourself into an upright position again and notice that there is a spansive rainbow arched up in the sky and another doorway that will allow you to walk on the inside of the rainbow as you journey to the other side of it. As you open the door and cross over the threshold on to this rainbow path you feel perfectly secure you are surrounded on all sides by the beautiful rainbow colors pulsating and beaming with waves of light. Your Angels and those that you have invited are walking with you. It is so warm and loving within this rainbow, experience each color as you continue to cross to the other side.

You approach the end and the doorway leads you into a large field of luscious green grass and trees. You are in a clearing that is surrounded on all sides by a forest.

The Angles have accompanied you and are beckoning you to stand in the very center of this field. As you walk and reach the center position you begin to see people starting to arrive and circle around you. At first only one or two, then hundreds, then thousands, it could actually be even millions.

Your Angels assist you to understand that each of these entities has come into contact with you within this live time or past lifetimes. As you look down at your body now you see that each one of these individuals is connected to you with an elastic cord. You are completely covered up and can barely move because of all of these cords that are attached to you.

The Angles are motioning to you to select a cord and simply start removing them one by one. You decide to start at your feet and work up. You unplug the cords from your feet and toes and ankles and they go reeling back to each individual that the cord was connected to. As you clear each area you are filled with the Christed Light that has been long waiting to return to you. Your feet and ankles are radiating and pulsing with this beautiful Christed Light that has returned to its rightful place. Beginning now at the lower leg, knee and shin disconnecting all, clear now and the Christed Light continues to flow upward. Disconnecting the thigh area the hips, waist and chest areas now. The light flows into those spaces and you are once again sensing the wholeness that was once yours. You continue to release the balance of the cords and after each release the Christed Light flows into that area and once again is emanating from it. The head and crown chakra are the last places and you disconnect those. You feel so wonderful and alive and vibrant now that these cords have all been removed.

You turn to all those gathered around you. They have tears of joy and release rolling down their faces, as do you. You thank them and they too are sensing a wonderful freedom and release and thank you in return for releasing them from those ties that you had together that no longer served yours or their higher good.

You bid them goodbye and tell them that you love them. The Angels lead your glowing radiating body back to the door of the Rainbow Bridge and you walk back across, a new lighter bounce in your step for you feel so much lighter and brighter now.

You open the doorway on the other side and bounce on to that glorious cloud once more. Oh how good it feels to be free. You enter the doorway back into your present life. Wiggle your fingers and toes and when you are ready open your eyes.

How do you feel?

Beloveds you are blessed beyond words and loved beyond measure.

I Am Archangel Michael, The Creator's Messenger of Love, Joy, Wisdom, Light, Peace & Grace.

What colors did you find yourself interacting with as you crossed over the Rainbow Bridge?

Chapter 18
<u>A Message From Archangel Michael</u>

<u>Remembrance of The Golden Light</u>

Greetings, Beautiful Beings of Light this season of December is one of many different moods upon the Earth Plane. For many this is a season of joy, celebration and anticipation of the coming new year. For some it is a season of aloneness, tears, pain, fear, lack and scarcity.

What do you think that it might be that makes some elated and some very sad. My precious Beloved Beings it is their feelings of being loved and cherished by The Creator and those about them.

Perhaps those that are alone have placed themselves into a mental box and indeed forgotten that they are with their very own Angels on a moment-by-moment basis. The visual eyes cannot see the Angels, but the heart's eyes <u>know</u> that the Angels are truly there. The veils are slowly dissolving and the re-membrance is coming back now. Ask your Angels to walk with you in each moment. Those that feel so painfully alone and lost give your Angels permission to come into your lives and assist you. Talk to them out loud as you would anyone else that you can physically see in the room for they are there my Beloveds. Tell them your feelings and those things that you would ask their assistance with. They only await your invitation to enfold you with their love and help. They truly are your gifts of assistance from The Creator.

There are many different levels of awakening and re-membering occurring on all levels, dimensions and within all aspects of each Beingness.

The last month's messages have been devoted to clearing old out dated programs, relationships, past connections all that no longer served the highest highest highest good of all concerned. The clearing is an ongoing process and is to be continued. There will always be a need to release because you are constantly changing and evolving. Each time you let go of a piece that no longer is of service you raise your vibration. You literally are becoming lighter and lighter.

As you become lighter and lighter your awareness is keener, things appear clearer and sharper. Colors become more vibrant. You find that you are focusing more on the beauty that The Creator has placed here for you and you feel The Creator's love much more intensely than before.

What you have been doing my Beautiful Light Warriors is clearing the debris from your energy fields so that The Creator's love can reach you more easily. It is very much like opening the door of a room that has been in total darkness. The light from the doorway sweeps in and begins to illume the room. The wider that you open the door the more light that is allowed to permeate the area displacing the darkness.

The clearing and releasing also allows the thought process to begin searching for new areas of interest and information that are coming forth from your remembrance of The Creator's love. You are all making such wonderful strides. Your lights are shining so

106

brightly as you work more and more to once again recognize the link to the you that is you.

Releasing the old and going within to find your answers is what this process is all about.

The energy fields around the physical Beingness are cleared and cleaned.

Another meditation gift.

I would ask you now to ask your Ego self to move aside and perch on your left shoulder. Invite your Higher Self to merge and integrate within your Beingness. These instructions are for the Higher self.

Find a quiet place where you will not be disturbed for a while. Sit or lie whichever is more comfortable for you. I ask that you relax the body.

Envision the Creator's protective white light coming down from the corner of the room and entering through your crown chakra and completely permeating your Beingness. Now see the light overflowing and completely permeating and filling all the room. You are now divinely protected and nothing can harm you without your permission.

The Creator has gifted you with another ray of light. This ray is Golden in color and begins to enter through the soles of your feet. It completely fills the physical vessel as it goes up through all the chakras and all parts of the Beingness all levels dimensions and aspects. Completely permeating all of the Beingness.

Your Beingness is radiating with the Golden light of transmutation.

107

Visualize yourself becoming lighter and lighter as if you were a balloon filled with helium. You sense you are journeying now and realize that you are traveling in the form that is really the you that is you. You can if you desire, see your physical vessel below just as you had left it. One of your guides is constantly with it. Do not be concerned about it, it is awaiting your return and is in perfection as you travel.

Sense yourself rising to the ceiling of the room.

Further rising above the rooftop of the house or whatever type structure you are in.

Further rising up into the skies.

Further rising into space.

As you are going up repeat to yourself " Rising in The Gold", "Rising in The Gold", "Rising in The Gold".

From a vantage point in space look back now and see the Earth Plane way beneath you. Feel your love for this beautiful blue ball, but remember that you are not of the Earth only an occupant of that plane of existence. You have been a spiritual being having a human experience.

Continue to rise. When you are guided to stop do so.

You might sense a presence in whatever way is appropriate for you. Ask them what would they have you know. Give them several minutes and if it is appropriate to receive the message it will come. If not know that it will, when the moment is right.

Thank the messenger and ask them to journey with you.

Continue to rise and repeat " Rising in the Gold", Rising in The Gold", Rising in The Gold".

You have reached a point within your awareness that seems so incredibly warm and energized, as you turn you are awash with the magnificence of The Creator.

You allow yourself totally to merger with The Creator. You remember this feeling from something far far far in your past. Oh the pure ecstasy and bliss, the joy and rapture that has just swept over you. You are filled with such amazement and grace.

You sense the you that is you expanding and becoming as wide and as full as the Universe. You have become the Whole, the One once again, All That Is, the I AM That I AM.

Repeat now " I AM GOLDEN LIGHT, I AM GOLDEN LIGHT, I AM GOLDEN LIGHT". Breathe in the Gold and relish in that glory.

Linger as long as you wish and when you sense it is time to return give The Creator one last hug and know that you will never be the same, for you have experienced The Creator's love one more time and remembered that this is HOME.

See the you that is really you descending back from the Creator from whence you came, back down through space, the skies, once again coming back down into the room, and gently re-entering the physical vessel that has been patiently awaiting your return.

You bring the physical vessel a gift of love for yourself and all that you encounter and such joy that you have just experienced and it will fill the physical vessel to over flowing.

Wiggle your fingers and your toes and fully allow yourself to completely come back into the Earth Plane before going about your activities.

I Am Archangel Michael, The Creator's Messenger of Love, Joy, Wisdom, Light, Peace & Grace.

Any Angel Messages Received ?

Chapter 19

A Message From Archangel Michael

The Gift of Manifesting Tools

Beloved Beings of light you have transversed the feared 2000-year change over and are now ready to forge ahead in search of your new year's path.

In truth you create anew in each moment. Each moment is new and in perfection with the Creator's Master Blue Print. What makes each moment unique and unto itself is the freedom of choice decisions that color each breath and each beat of your heart.

Communication has been provided about thoughts and how they do in fact manifest into their own realties. Communications have been shared, due to this manifestation capability involving the Laws of Cause and Effect, reminding you that which you fear is drawn near. The importance of Intent has been echoed many times.

The steps to realization and need to identify that, which needed releasing, has been shared. The tools have been given of meditation, visualization and examples of ways in which the you that you are can begin to clear away the old out dated areas that no longer serve your highest good.

Beautiful Beings Of Light your essence is gleaming and the rays are reaching throughout the Universe. Your intent has been heard many times over. The Angels are singing your praises of joy and exultation. The love that has been shared with the Universe is being returned to you in a pulsating fashion for your next step on your evolutionary ladder.

Allow that special pulsating vibration of love to permeate all parts of your Beingness. See it as a glorious pink pulsating cocoon in constant motion around your Beingness all levels dimensions and aspects. This pink energy is pure love. It is more potent than anything that you remember on the Earth Plane and it is coming directly do you from The Creator. You are the Creator's Perfection and deserve only the very finest of all things. The Creator loves you beyond words or measure.

Creating my Light Warriors is a gift that you <u>all</u> share. This is a common denominator within each entity on the Earth Plane. That which is created is the focus of your differences and separations and how it affects all that it touches. A forgotten moment, that you are who you are, can create within the blink of the eye through each thought your own heaven or your own desolate in escapable chasm.

Thoughts cannot be taken lightly. As you journey deeper within yourself this remembrance will become more real for you. Your awareness will begin to bring you more and more insights in how you have been creating your own part within the Earth Plane Play.

Charting a course for each new moment with the realization that you are in control of your world requires new tools to work with.

With your permission this Messenger would like to take you on a new journey. The purest and highest of intent is necessary on this sojourn. The exercises shared are to be used with the utmost of care and only with the deepest of love for yourself and All That Is.

You are going forward with the meditation demonstrates your acceptance of responsibility for your own actions and decision of free choice to walk farther on your spiritual path.

If you have a special crystal that you would like to work with during this meditation, please obtain it now and hold it in your left hand.

Find a comfortable spot where you will not be disturbed for a while. Sit or lie down whichever is more comfortable for you. You will be using a lot of energy for this adventure so you might like to cover the physical body with a light covering to keep it warm and distraction free if you are in a cool place.

From the corner of the room, visualize a white beam of light that has emanated directly from the Creator and now from the corner of the room it travels and enters your crown chakra. Visualize this light permeated all parts of your Beingness all levels dimensions and aspects. See it completely filling your Beingness and now radiating out from you to all parts of the room and all parts of the area you are occupying. It permeates everything. You are now divinely protected and only those things that you have given permission to (on any level of your Beingness) can penetrate that protective barrier.

I'll accompany you with your permission. Invite those that you would like on this journey to gather with you wherever you are located at the moment. Invite your Angels if you are comfortable doing that, your spiritual family, guides and any special heavenly entities that have meaning for you.

You are all gathered now. Ask your conscious mind to remain behind and perch on your left shoulder. It is to only be a spectator and witness on this venture. Request your Higher Self to fully merge with you at this time. Feel its energy and beauty filling you completely.

See a door form within your Heart Chakra; this is the entryway that is to be used for this meditation. The door handle is being turned, you cross the threshold into a corridor. An elevator door is open awaiting your arrival. You enter the elevator and notice that the button for the eleventh (11) level has been illuminated.

You begin ascending and ascending feeling your vibrations rising higher and higher with each level passed. Each level also brings a lighter feeling,

The elevator stops and the doors open you see that you are on a white cloud. You step out onto the cloud and notice that there is a rainbow directly overhead. It is so very beautiful. Odd but at this level you can feel not just see each color that the rainbow is showing you. Concentrate of whatever color feels the best for you at this time. Let that color wrap its vibration around you.

Notice off to your right a small sitting area with nothing around it. You are drawn to it and walk over. You notice as you walk that you really aren't walking but floating. Gliding with ease and grace with each thought to move forward. The physical parts don't have to work here. It is pure thought that moves the entity from one location to the next.

Your invited guests are motioning to you to take a seat. They surround you in a circle. Take a close look at them all with your heart eyes. Their colors are so sharp and vibrant here. Never before have you seen such a thing. Their beauty is breath taking. They are glowing and their colors are pulsating all around them.

Try touching one that you have invited. Remember to think touch and it will be accomplished the physical form isn't necessary at this level. Feel their vibrations.

One of them hands you a mirror. You look in the mirror and there you truly are. (Remember that if you do not see anything in the mirror at this time that it is only because this is not your time to see this image, it will come when your time is appropriate). It surprises you, that a physical form is not reflecting back to you now. You are seeing your radiant light being that you truly are.

You might notice that there is a color of the essence that you are seeing as well. The color vibration denotes your family origin. If this interests you research it upon your return.

Your invited guests remind you that you have your special crystal in your left hand. Look deeply into the crystal. Visualize yourself and guests entering the crystal itself. Your essence is now floating around in this beautiful crystal. Take a seat in the middle of the crystal floor. At this time, switch the crystal to your right hand. You sense that you are to form a thought within your Heart chakra of the most pristine purest peaceful place that you want to reside in.

You are directed to have the thought travel from your Heart Chakra, to the Third Eye Chakra exit through the Third Eye and out the top terminator point of this crystal that you are sitting in. As you are transmitting this thought through the designated routing you sense that you are to also create a tone and with that tone form the word "Ah" singing the tone as the thought travels it's outlined course into the Universe.

You are sensing that you are to hold this thought and continue this tone of "Ah" as long as it feels appropriate. As you continue the repetitions of this process your enter vision is watching this process. The energy is traveling from your Heart Chakra out through the Third Eye and then traveling through the crystal terminator point accompanied by the Tone and sound formed "Ah".

It looks like a line of golden energy pulsating out in waves. It is going directly out into the Universe in pulsating waves of the purest golden energy you have ever seen. This is amazing you sense.

Look at what this essence that is me is doing. This is the creation process this essence is remembering all the times that it has done this before. This is exciting the awareness floods in as the remembrance returns with the knowing that has always been there.

The understanding that each thought that goes out creates what the thought captured is indeed returning to your remembrance.

You return the crystal to your left hand when you feel it is appropriate and your creation process has come to a close.

When you sense that it is appropriate ask your invited guests to return with you out through the crystal floating back into the elevator. The elevator starts to descend. With each level you begin to feel heavier and heavier as your physical material self becomes more present within your realm.

The elevator doors open again within the corridor of your Heart Chakra and you remember that you must now physically tell yourself to move your feet at this level to exit the elevator. You turn the handle on the door and re-enter your physical vessel that has been awaiting your return. One of your Guardian Angels has been with it since your journey.

You being to wiggle your fingers and toes and re-orient yourself within your surroundings. You may feel a bit tired and drained. Creating at that level uses a tremendous amount of energy. Be kind to yourself and allow the physical body to re-adjust before continuing your day.

You have brought the remembrance of this adventure back with you. You realize now how potent that each thought can be.

Ask your Angels to assist you in identifying those times when your thoughts are leading into destructive or not higher serving actions. Should you find yourself noticing this negative trend immediately turn your attention to the most beautiful thing you can remember. Ask your Angels to have the thought cleared from all levels dimensions and aspects of your Beingness immediately. Know that it has been done and let it go.

Beloved Beautiful Beings of Light, *I Am Archangel Michael, The Creator's Messenger of Love, Joy, Wisdom, Light, Peace & Grace.*

Describe The Pristine Place You Envisioned

Chapter 20

A Message From Archangel Michael

The Test and The Creator's Lap

Beautiful Beings of Light, you are shinning so brightly are you not.

The year has started off with minimal trauma that was predicted with the millennium roll over. Are you surprised?

My Beloveds remember that predictions are just that, possibilities that have not materialized into reality because they were not the chosen possibilities.

Isn't it wonderful that the majority of the Earth Plane chose not to have the catastrophes of the Y2K come forth to embellish their lives and begin a new year?

More and more are coming forth to break the chains of the old belief systems by not selecting and embracing the outcomes just because someone else said it would be so.

We are so proud of your accomplishments. Feel our energies as we give each of you a spiritual hug and tell you job well done!

Tears of joy come to our eyes when we see that the past chains that have bound you are breaking and freeing you from the bondage that you felt you were doomed to follow just because others did.

The choirs of Angels sing your praises when we see the support that you are gathering one to another to help you walk your path upright and empowered.

Your spiritual family gathers around you even though you cannot see them and rejoices at each decision you make in a new direction.

Beloved Beings of Light there is so much joy for you to re-member and re-discover by just remaining within the Earth Plane to accomplish each of your missions.

The eyes of the heart and ears of the heart are daily becoming more in tuned to the beauty that you initially arrived in, so very very very long ago. This was before each of you started on your numerous reincarnations that did nothing but bring you more and more density, tears and blood shed for imagined causes to fight.

Oh the stories that the mass consciousness did weave to justify the death and destruction within this experiment. It was because you forgot your true form and essence and listening to someone else's reality that said it was so; therefore you bought into the imaged drama that has been occurring within this Earth Plane for eons.

With each tear that the Earth Mother has wept, The Creator returned to her more and more pink love light. With each prayer that has been sent forth, The Creator has been sending more and more golden light to awaken the Angels that you truly are.

The golden light has become so very strong now that the Earth Plane is taking on new radiance. We thank you for awakening and hearing the Earth Mother's cry and The Creator's call to return this Plane to The Creator's pristine brilliance in which it was initially created. This beautiful blue and green ball will once again exemplify its original pure essence of energy. The Creator only creates excellence and perfection; it is to this state that the Earth Mother will return to her highest essence, perfection and new higher vibration.

The more you journey within, the more you will indeed awaken and become more aware. This is why each time you are gifted with a meditation to draw you back into your source of divine guidance. It is there that you will be given your most accurate information. It is there that your questions will be appropriately answered.

You are so individualized and special that the appropriate answer for one would not be the appropriate answer for all. As with the Earth Mother so it is with you, The Creator only creates excellence and perfection, so too will you return to your original state of the purest of energies by going within and stripping away all that no longer serves and release all that is not for the highest good. Your past density layers begin dissolving and only the very best of experience will remain and come forward with your evolution.

Have compassion for yourself and others and understand that each has much to work on to bring each essence to the next rung of the spiral.

The test my Warriors of Light will come within the still quiet moments of your own psyche when your ego brings forth doubts to hinder your path. It will tell you that you are physical and it will tell you that you are not an Angel and it will tell you all the negative things that it knows will punch your buttons.

The test is, will you allow yourself to believe it, because your friends, family, fathers and fore fathers believed it, or will you grasp what your heart, soul and higher guidance are telling you and reach out for that branch when you are within the swirling waters of doubt, allowing The Creator to draw you towards your true identity and spiritual path of safety. Will you allow The Creator to encircle you within it glorious golden energy and wrap you in the love that has been waiting for you to re-member it?

Let us walk together my Beautiful Beings of Light, with your permission, and journey within to where your truth and wisdom reside.

Find a quiet place where you will not be disturbed for a while. Sit or lie down whichever is more comfortable for you. Cover yourself with a light blanket if you feel that your physical body might be chilled during this journey. Allow yourself to be free from distraction.

Ask your ego self to step aside for this journey. Tell it that it will be the observer only and will be allowed to perch on your left shoulder. Visualize this ego self as a symbol if you wish, but know that it will heed your instruction.

Close your eyes, give your intention and permission for only those things that are for your very highest good to be in your presence. Feel the white light of protection from The Creator beginning in the corner of the room as it starts to permeate all parts of your Beingness. It is circulating from The Creator entering through your feet up through your entire body exiting from your crown chakra and returning to The Creator in a circular motion. It then emanates out filling the room with only the very highest energy essence and divine grace allowing you perfect ease and peace.

With your permission feel the presence of your Angels, Guides and Spiritual Family; all are gathered round you, as am I, if you desire it to be so.

Visualize your heart chakra and see yourself walking around within it. You see the door and today you are going to inscribe on that door with golden letters these words "The Door To Your Highest Guidance Within". There is only one door so never allow your ego to tell you otherwise.

Open the door, you find that there is a white marble hall way on the other side. In this hallway you see to your right a clear hollow crystal tube with escalator steps going up, there is an elevator to the left and a table with a key. There is also a flower in a vase on the table. What is the flower setting on your table? What color is it? Remember these things and when you return, look up the meaning for yourself for there are messages within these two for you.

Pick up the key and take the escalator.

You feel the you that is really you rising up out of the physical form that you thought was you. You are rising up out of your room, continuing higher out of your house, higher still out of your town; continue your escalator trip higher still out of your Earth Plane.

See the beautiful blue and green ball below and see it glowing with the golden light that all the light workers have so labored with love to bring forth. The escalator is still moving going past the seventh level now, the eighth, the ninth, the tenth, the eleventh and stops at the twelfth level.

As you have journeyed through each phase have you noticed that you have become less visible and the density has become lighter and lighter. Your essence is now very much like a flame or ball of translucent golden energy. You don't even have to step off the escalator you simply think movement and it is done. You are floating off as you tell your essence to exit at this level. In front of you there is a golden gate.

Take your key and open the gate. The key will now remain in this gate for you always for you have remembered the way and can return at any time. Inside the gate is a high crystal palace. You find that as you float along that there is a wondrous garden all around with all kinds of foliage, flowers and animals that you have never physically seen on the Earth Plane.

Return here and explore sometime if you wish but for now journey on down the path. You have an appointment to keep.

Continue floating through the garden and as you approach the palace doors look up in the blue heavens and see all types of white birds that you've never seen before.

One lands on you and gifts you with a flower; notice the color is not one that you normally see. You take the flower from its mouth and it says, "Welcome! Welcome!, it has been so long since we've seen you". You notice that tears of joy are flowing down from the bird's eyes and it flies away.

You are at the door now and it is very large, looks very heavy, but as you turn the handle with your intention you notice it opens with ease.

You step inside, the colors from the crystal construction are refracting within allowing the colors to dance freely all around your essence. A golden light is emanating from all aspects of this building.

The Angels are all around singing in glorious chorus such exquisite notes and sounds. A feeling of total peace is present, it reminds you of something from your far past. You are guided to the middle of the structure to a group of steps that lead up to what appears to be a huge golden chair.

You can't see it really because the light that is glowing from it is so bright that it is almost blinding. You look away trying to clear your vision.

A voice emanating from The Creator's Golden Essence says, "Come here My Child". "You are right on time for our appointment".

You feel a little unsure of what to do. Again The Creator's voice guides you, "Come here My Child, walk up the steps and enter My essence" "You will remember this essence My Child, for it will feel like you are sitting on My lap surrounded by My Love". "My Child you have been within My Golden Essence Energy Lap so many times before, the memories will come flooding back now if you allow it to be so".

The Creator's voice soothingly says, "Do not be afraid, you have been away for a long time My Darling One." "I have missed you and love you beyond what any of your physical words can describe." " Float into My Essence Little One, at the last step there and We will once again merge as One Entity for that is All That Is".

Directing The Creator continues," That is it just float into My Golden Essence and allow it to engulf you, surrender to its peace." "Think of it My Little One as just opening your physical hands and allowing what was firmly clasped there to be free". "Let the Golden Light just wash over you as you sit here on My Golden Energy Lap". "Allow Me to embrace you and merge My peace and love within you."

The Creator asks" What are the tears for My Beloved Little One, you are re-membering now aren't you?" " Talk to me Loved One what would you have Me know on this visit Child?" Give yourself some time here and tell The Creator what it is that is of greatest concern to you here.

Listen to The Creator; hear the whispers of guidance in your ears. Be patient with yourself if you do not hear anything at this time the guidance will come when it is appropriate.

The Creator comfortingly says " There There Little One, There There, allow the love energy to wipe away the tears be them of joy or sorrow". Feel The Creator rocking you back and forth comforting you as you remain on The Creator Golden Energy Lap.

The Creator continues" Leave the concerns and all with Me My Child, allow Me to help you in whatever is for your highest concern". "Know that I AM always with you Little One within your heart and that you but only have to call on Me and I AM there."

The Creator reluctantly says " It is time for you to return now My Child your mission is not done, be at peace, show your love and compassion to all that cross your path for We are All One within this Essence."

You step back through The Creator's Gold Energy Essence as you disengage from The Creator, your heart is singing and you feel lighter than you have in years. You know that nothing is what it seems; you have remembered that all the physical is but an illusion.

As you float back down the steps you vow to yourself to never allow so much separation to happen again. You float back out the door and back through the garden. You notice that your essence has retained much of the Golden Light from the merging with The Creator and you are being allowed to bring it back with you.

You float back to the escalator steps and begin the descent into your heart chakra. You step from the escalator back into the white marble hallway. You add the flower that the bird gifted you with to the flower within the vase.

The flower's addition is now bringing the Golden Essence to the flower that was originally in the vase. You see this Golden Light is something that will touch all that you touch, as it was gifted to you for this purpose. So as you interact with others, part of your gifted Golden Essence will be shared with them as well.

You are coming back into your physical presence now. You are feeling energized and revitalized. You wiggle your fingers and your toes. Be gentle with yourself this day you have been on a very long journey, the effects need to have time to settle in place here on the Earth Plane. You have much to do today within your mission. You have brought back the tools of The Creator's Golden Essence, love and guidance to begin anew.

Gift your Golden Essence to others and know that it will allow them to walk their higher path.

Re-member Beautiful Beings Of Light that you may travel back to The Creator's Palace at any time. The Creator's presence is carried within you, and is your highest source of guidance. The Creator's whispers maybe heard at any time. A request for help from The Creator for the divine comfort, counsel, and direction are but a prayer away.

I Am Archangel Michael, The Creator's Messenger of Love, Joy, Wisdom, Light, Peace & Grace.

A Message From My Guardian Angel
By Carolyn Ann O'Riley

While all the earth is still and at peace,
I watch over you all night as you sleep.
I touch your hair with my Angel wings.
Fill your head with Angelic Host Singing.

My love for you is unconditional and everlasting
I'll be with you always even after your passing.
I stand in guard over your presence today
And watch as you kneel to God to pray.

My time with you is never ending.

© From the book "Go Within Feel The Love" by
Carolyn Ann O'Riley

About the Author
Carolyn Ann O'Riley

Carolyn has been channeling Archangel Michael's messages for humanity globally since 1998.

Prior to 2009 Carolyn's day job was in Corporate Management. After eleven years of working during the day and channeling at night she finally said enough is enough and is devoting her remaining years of service to Archangel Michael's channeling work along with her Life Coaching and Hypnotherapy practice. Carolyn is finding that her Life Coaching and Hypnotherapy works hand in hand with Archangel Michael's mission, for her, of helping others learn to go back within themselves to find their own most perfect answers.

Carolyn is Certified Hypnotic Life Coach and Certified Hypnotist. She is also Certified in Past Life Regression Hypnosis as well as Life Between Lives Regression Hypnosis.

The Author has had a passion for writing and drawing since she was a small child. This has proven to be her spiritual mission during this lifetime.

Her articles & poetry have been published in magazines, books, journals, within greeting cards and many other types of media.

The Author's artwork and designs have been exhibited in shows as well as used by such prestigious establishments as the famed Mansion on Turtle   Creek.

Archangel Michael's messages have traveled around the world and back again again many times. They are being translated into other languages and published within many other formats.

The books, writings, recordings, and art are dedicated to The Creator and The Creator's Messenger, Archangel Michael. They are for all ages, and peoples, no matter the race, creed, origin, religion, or culture. These books and messages are from the Universal Spiritual Heart and written in the Universal Spiritual Language of Love. They are appropriate for All.

Other Books That You Might Enjoy

Archangel Michael Course Book
The Remembrance of I AM An Inner Journey of Self
Discovery A Channeled Course From Archangel Michael
ISBN 1-4116-6886-3

(e-book) The Remembrance of I AM
ISBN 978-1-105-62004-1

The Collection of Archangel Michael Speaks Series
The Journey Within Book I
ISBN 1-4116-7931-8

(e-book) The Journey Within Book I
ISBN 978-1-105-59326-0

And The Angels Walk Beside You Book II
ISBN 1-4116-9348-7

(e-book) An The Angels Walk Beside You Book II
ISBN 978-1-106-59513-4

When We Quiet Our Fears We Find Love Book III
ISBN 978 -1-4116-6486-9

(e-book) When We Quiet Our Fears We Find Love
ISBN 978-1-105-61163-6

The Path To Discovery Book IV
ISBN 1-4116-5251-7

(e-book) The Path To Discovery Book IV
ISBN 978-1-105-61219-0

Going Up! Hold On To Your Angels Book V
ISBN 978-0-557-07166-1

(e-book) Going Up! Hold On To Your Angels
ISBN 978-1-105-61698-3

Note To Self: Ask for More Angels Book VI
ISBN 978-1-257-09328-1

(e-book) Note To Self Ask for More Angels
ISBN 978-1-105-61951-9

And The Angels Are With You Now Book VII
ISBN 978-1-105-79352-3

(e-book) And The Angels Are With You Now Book VII
ISBN 978-1-105-80887-6

For inspirational reading here is a true life story:
The Lady of Court Square The Biography of Eva Caroline
Whitaker Davis A Lady of Courage That Would Not Accept
Defeat
ISBN 1-4116-4808-0

(e-book) The Lady of Court Square
ISBN 978-1-105-62312-7

(The Lady of Court Square is not a channeled work but written
by Carolyn Ann O'Riley and is available from the above book
sources as well)

The Archangel's Pen
Carolyn Ann ORiley
18794 Vista Del Sol
Dallas, Texas 75287-4023 USA
214-232-7199 Phone

We invite you to view Archangel Michael's monthly messages as they are posted to our web site.

http://www.carolynannoriley.com Web site
e-mail address: To write to Carolyn
channel333@sbcglobal.net

Your Angel Journal
A Very Special Place To Keep Your Own Angel Experiences